Countdo

a play

Spaceman   **Grandma**   **Control One**

Control Two   **Lady**   **Crowd**

Nelson

Control One:

The rocket is ready, Spaceman.

Spaceman:

Goodbye, Grandma. Goodbye.

Grandma:

Now don't get into any danger. And don't fly too fast.

Control Two:

Hurry up, Spaceman. You'll be late.

Spaceman:

Yes, yes, all right. Grandma, I have to go.

Grandma:

Brush your teeth before you go to bed. Don't eat any lollies. Have an apple twice a day.

Spaceman:

Yes, yes, Grandma.

Control One:

Spaceman, are you ready for countdown?

Spaceman:

Look, Grandma, you're making me late.

3

Control Two:

Spaceman, you'd better be quick.

Grandma:

Don't forget to wash behind your ears. And, when you get to the moon, wear something warm. You don't want to get a cold.

Spaceman:

I'll remember, Grandma.

Control One:

Spaceman, you'll have to come *now*.

Spaceman:

Sorry, Grandma. I'm off!

Lady:

There's the spaceman! He's getting into the rocket.

Crowd:

Goodbye, Spaceman. Goodbye, goodbye.

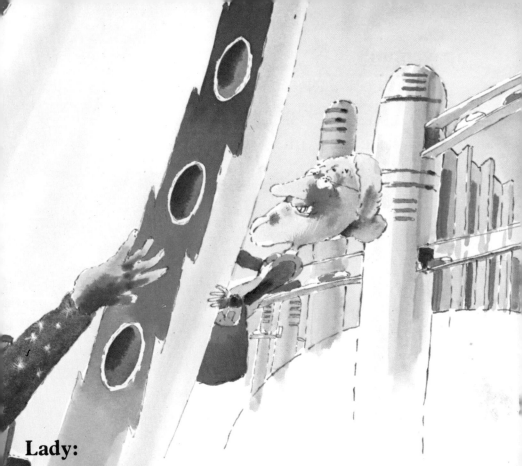

Lady:

They're ready for countdown.

Control Two:

Ten, nine, eight, seven, six, five, four, three, two, one, BLAST-OFF!

Crowd:

Three cheers for the spaceman!
Hip-hip-hooray!   Hip-hip-hooray!   Hip-hip-hooray!

People go home.

Spaceman:

Ah! Off at last! I was afraid I'd never get away from Grandma. *(He pushes buttons.)* How nice and quiet it is up here — all by myself.

Sounds of footsteps.

Spaceman:

Wha-at's that? Who is it?

Grandma:

It's me, dear.

Spaceman:

Grandma! What are you doing here?

Grandma:

I've come to look after you. I'll see that you brush your teeth and comb your hair. I'll wash your space-suit when it gets dirty.

Spaceman:

Oh no!

Grandma:

I'll cook you lots of vegetables, so you don't get skinny. Won't that be nice?

Spaceman:

But I don't like vegetables.

Grandma:

We'll be together for three whole months.

Spaceman:

Oh no, we won't.

Grandma:

What's that you're putting on me?

Spaceman:

Your parachute, Grandma. Good bye!